# REVIVED

## 21-DAY DEVOTIONAL JOURNAL

*A Guide to Motivating, Encouraging and Uplifting Your Life.*

-Kierra Alderman-

Copyright © 2019. Kierra Alderman All Rights Reserved.

All rights reserved. No part of this book may be reproduced or transmitted in any form or by any means, electronic or mechanical, including photocopying, recording, or by an information storage and retrieval system - except by a reviewer who may quote brief passages in a review to be printed in a magazine or newspaper - without permission in writing from the publisher or author.

Unless otherwise indicated, scripture was taken from the Holy Bible King James Version (KJV)- Public.

ISBN: 978-1-7330657-2-6


Email: bolempoerment@gmail.com
Website: www.bolempowerment.com
Facebook: @bolempowerment
Twitter: @Kiealderman
Instagram; @Kiealderman

# DEDICATION

I dedicate this book to anyone who has ever believed that they were greater beyond their wildest dreams. To anyone who's had a desire to do more in life, or become more in life, and all you needed was for someone to believe in you and encourage you.

-This is dedicated to you!

## COMMITMENT

As excited as I am to have you purchase this book, I want to encourage you not to sign your name below until you are sick and tired of being sick and tired. Only then will you truly have a desire to stay committed on this journey. Please know that you can fool me, you can even fool yourself, but you cannot fool God.

I _____ vow to commit myself to this 21-Day devotional challenge. I vow to adhere to the readings and the assignments outlined within this reading.

## TABLE OF CONTENTS

| | |
|---|---|
| **Dedication** | 3 |
| **Commitment** | 4 |
| **Introduction** | 7 |
| Day 1: Who Does God Says You Are? | 16 |
| Day 2: Be Awakened | 25 |
| Day 3: Limitless | 33 |
| Day 4: Goal Getter ~Focus On The Prize | 40 |
| Day 5: Interested | 46 |
| Day 7: Be Consistent | 53 |
| Day 8: Purposed Prayer | 59 |
| Day 9: Become Thirsty | 67 |
| Day 10: Wonderful Giving | 73 |
| Day 6: Giving Up Isn't An Option | 79 |
| Day 11: Positioned In His Presence | 88 |
| Day 12: Take A Stand | 93 |
| Day 13: Be Righteous | 98 |
| Day 14: Walk In Love | 103 |

| | |
|---|---|
| Day 15: Think Big | 110 |
| Day 16: Be Disciplined | 115 |
| Day 17: Be Fearless | 121 |
| Day 18: Be Strong | 127 |
| Day 19: Being Content | 133 |
| Day 20: Fall In Love | 138 |
| Day 21: Harvest Time | 143 |
| **You Are** | 147 |
| **Concluding Prayer** | 148 |
| **Acknowledgements** | 151 |

# Introduction

In opening, I want you to know that you just signed up and committed to do work. This is going to be an interactive devotional. Your thought process will be challenged, molded and stretched, but I promise to guide you through this process of feeling more empowered and encouraged.

To begin, I want you to know that you are fearfully and wonderfully made. You've been created by design and instilled with purpose. There is absolutely no one who can replace you or your gifts. It is for this reason that it's essential for you to do all you can do to become all that you will be. When God created you, he knew you, and he knew you had all the potential to be extraordinary. After all, you were created in the image of a God!

> *"And God said, Let us make man in our image, after our likeness: and let them have dominion over the fish of the sea, over the fowl of the air, over the cattle, and over all the earth, and over every creeping thing that creepeth upon the earth."*
> **- Genesis 1:26**

Did you read that? I don't just mean skim over it, but really read it, and take a moment to allow the scripture to marinate? God adored man so much that he designed and molded us in his own image, the image of the almighty. No other creation, including the angels, were said to be created in God's image. That small subconscious voice that nags at you, telling you that you were designed for more and you deserve more; its right. You were and you do!  He loved everything he created. He gave you, as a special creation, dominion over all the other things he created. Can you can see how unique your nature is and how spectacular your future is in God? He's a God with plans and purpose and if you were fortunate enough to be his special design, then you should never doubt what your life holds in store. When you allow God to order your steps, there is nothing in existence that can stop you. Sure, there will be weapons formed against you because the enemy has a job to do, and he has never missed a day of work. God never said that the weapon wouldn't be formed, he said that the weapon will not prosper.

If you can imagine just how great and how powerful God is, you can begin to imagine your future being secured allowing you to reach your goal. There is a power shift that begins to happens when you realize that your goal is not only fathomable, it is also achievable. It will give you the motivation that you need to not only cease the opportunity of today, but to also tomorrow.

God is love, and everything he has created was formed out of his unique love and desire for a relationship with his creation. He desires for you to see him and be hopeful in everything you are going through. Like any other creator, he wants you to know why you were built, and what you were built to do. He wants you to embrace yourself with the same love he has shown unto you. Love who you are, love your unique qualities, embrace self-love, and be pleased with everything you have. Out of the little things you possess, God can manifest greater than you could ever desire.

Man was created to be bold, courageous, and confident, despite the fact you may be going through the most challenging moments of your life. Know that when you seem as though you are going through day after day, fight after fight, your breakthrough is on the horizon and the enemy is hoping you give up before the break of day. In order to have an effectual transformation, we must begin to think through the spirit and the comforter and not the flesh man. There are many issues you will face in life. In fact, it's scriptural that we would have to go through many obstacles, challenges, and sufferings, but it is also scriptural that we come out victorious, guaranteed. If you are going through tough times, you should be at ease to see where to solve your issues and be confident that you are coming out safe because you are not ordinary. You are full of potentials and strengths and are capable of doing great things. Problems are not meant to bring us down; they are meant to reveal to you that you know a problem solver. As long as you never give in and continue to push forward, you will always see the bright side of every challenge or situation you are going through.

The more you choose to channel this mindset and realize challenges are designed to bring out the best in us and are necessary to elevate us higher in the journey of life, the more you will stop running from your test and will actually start seeking them out. When there are challenges it means you are being put to the test. If you can pass the test of man without fail, you will be not all the wiser but have an advantage to help those who are still falling into the enemy's test.

That brings me to the essence of this devotional. It is to help you discover yourself and know how to get out of your comfort zone and be the best you that you are destined to be. I want you to know the only limitation to your greatness, your breakthrough, your deliverance, is and has always been within you. The courage you need to get out of your situation, circumstance, or mindset to become the best you, has been made readily available to you since your creation. It will remain silent unless you summon out the greatness that dwells within and claim what God has already promised you.

Let's look at miners for a second. The gold they are mining will always be underground and beneath the surface. Away from the present eye to be held if the miners fail to mine it. This is the same for your gifts. They will continue to lie dormant if you do not spiritually mine them. Do you know how valuable gold is in our generation today? Yet it has no value when it is buried underground.

Actively participating in this journal is the declaration to the enemy that you are going to make the conscious and spirit lead decision to be empowered and to transition into your purpose. This only works if you activate your belief and follow the steps in the journal. I am here to help you come out of whatever you have been going through. To encourage you to break away from whatever is restraining you and to aid you in overcoming whatever has been keeping you bound. It is time to mine your gold! When you have completed this book, you will be able to speak against the enemy, defy all the odds and barriers you were facing, and begin militating towards your destiny and your purpose in life. Remember that when God created you, he created you in likeness, and you possess grand abilities because of this. Even Jesus said that these things that I do you can also do and do them greater. This means you are full of power, strength, courage, and capability to persevere wherever and in whatever you aspire to do.

I want to be clear that this book is not going to instill something new into you. It is going to provide you with the tools necessary to mine your gold. This devotional journal is going to be our joint effort to help manifest your determination to get to your next destination. Again, Joint Effort! I have taken the first step by giving us an outline of our 21-day devotional journey to your transformation, so please make use of this powerful journal. Write in it, highlight it, tear out pages, stick them around your office, in your purse, and even hang them on your mirror! (I would write sticky notes on mirror and fridge all the time) I truly believe it will help you become a more empowered individual. Each day on our 21-day journey is specially equipped with words of wisdom that will stir up the gift lying dormant within you so that you can confidently face every challenge that arises on the way to your destiny.

Every day is full of both positives and negatives, but only the empowered will grasp that it's a difference in the two. This is truly the mindset of the beholder. For there is nothing that we encounter that catches God by surprise and there is nothing that he cannot orchestrate to work in for our good in the long run. You have to choose your mindset and make the choice that you do not want to limit yourself. You no longer want to focus on the bad and terrible things in each day. Or wallow in defeat and remain slave to despair. Today is the day you declare that you will have a better day. If you don't you will soon condition yourself into accepting that being stagnant is your fate and that complacency is all you were designed for. This is the mindset that prevents people from rising in life. If you want your life to be empowered, you must first choose to think and believe you are empowered. Break the victim mindset. I want this book to teach you that you have to stop compromising your standards and to sacrifice for your goals. This journal will be an invitation for the lord to endow you with the abundance.

My aim is that after this devotional journey, you will be ready to take your place among the giants of this generation through the unveiling your hidden inner gold. It is my desire that day by day, chapter by chapter, and step by step, God reveals your purpose and your calling and that you are motivated and courageous enough to pursue it. My prayer is that you make a daily effort to uplift and unveil your inner spirit man to fuel you on your journey to your overflow. Please be sure to TAKE THIS ONE DAY AT A TIME!!!! If you are anything like me, that will be the most challenging part because I love to work ahead. I truly encourage you to take this one day at a time and instead read the daily devotional as many times as you can every day. This will aid you in staying steadfast, and diligent, and persuade you to listen to that inner voice of wisdom. Are you ready for a renewed mindset? Are you ready to be revived?

# Day 1: Who Does God Say You Are?

> *"Before I formed thee in the belly I knew thee; and before thou camest forth out of the womb I sanctified thee, and I ordained thee a prophet unto the nations."*
>
> **-Jeremiah 1:5**

Today's devotional will concentrate on focusing on who God says you are and letting go of who man says you are. There is only one outlook on your life that you need to be concerned with, and that is God's outlook. You have got to break away from who your parents, your spouse and children, your employer, and even from who your church says you are and focus solely on who God declares you are. This, and this alone is the only truth about you. It is challenging for someone to say that they know who we are, when honestly at times, we don't even know who we are ourselves. Don't believe me? Have you ever done or said something that was completely out of character, and surprised yourself? Have you ever looked back over your life and asked, why was I head over hills for that person? How did I stay in that toxic situation? Have you endured something that was meant to break you in every way shape or form, but instead you came out with a praise report and realized that you were stronger than you imagined? None of those? How about change your mind 100 times about what you want to do in life? The truth is we are constantly evolving and developing and thus forever changing. This is why only God truly knows who we are and what we are capable of evolving to. When God says yes for you, nobody can say no. Even though the words of doubters and discouragers are coming at you strong, know that their words are invalid and irrelevant. As long as you are pleasing in God'ss eyesight, you will always rise above them and leave them wondering why you are so favored. Your focus should be tailored towards God's decision and outlook for your life and not mans. Your question should be, "Who does God say that I am currently and who is it that he wants me to evolve to?" Your purpose and validation can only come from your creator. His desire for you is to reach your goals in life and glorify his holy name.

When you are confused about your life and your ambitions and when you think you are not getting things right the way they should be, what comes to the mind of a typical person is the thought of giving up and quitting. This leads to discouragement. This is exactly where the enemy wants you. Defeated, discouraged, and nonetheless wiser of knowing you are capable of turning things around. I assure you quitting won't help you prevent the problems from coming. On the contrary, it will invite the enemy to continue to release havoc in your life. The only solution you need in these moments of distress is to focus on your declaration from God. Reflect on who he called you to be. Did he make you weak? Did He make you feeble? Did He make you powerless? Did He make you without direction? While you reflect, also remember you were created in his image.

We often hear that we are a reflection of our parents. This is true, but we are also a reflection of the God we serve. If you are powerless, then you serve a powerless God. Does that statement rub you the wrong way? Or does it make you realize that you have more power over your situation than you realized? I stated in the introduction that this was going to have to be a shift in your thought process, a renewed mindset. When you recognize and acknowledge that God is in control and all you have to do is endure, you will begin realizing exactly what God is commanding to the storms in your life.

He told prophet Jeremiah that he knew him even when he's still in the womb and has ordained him a prophet to all nations. The purpose of God for your life is beyond our everyday reasoning or comprehension. In fact, his ways are not our ways, and they are far greater than our ways. God sees situations and circumstances we are currently going through and the ones we will go through in the future, but he also sees the outcome. Think about a fight you would fight differently, harder, smarter, faster, longer or whatever if you knew ultimately you would win the fight. All God wants is for us to be at peace with him and to always rely on him in any situation we find ourselves in, as he desires what is best for us.

Who does God say you are? is the question that needs to be deeply embedded in your heart in order to create a revived mindset. All he said and he's still saying about you is that you are unique, you are a royal priesthood, you are powerful, you are full of strength, you are brave. You can become whatever and whoever you desire, if you don't allow yourself to get in the way of you. Even in his chastisement, God still favors us. His words are always everlasting and built with our victory in mind. Jeremiah 29 lets us know that God has a plan in place for us. His grace is sufficient and will be heirs to the kingdom if we faint not. We were born because we each possess a gift, a piece to the puzzle. God is waiting for us to ignite with it, in an effort to stir up the next person's gift. God declares that there's something good that will come out of our lives and that every day we are still above ground is purposed. Before he formed us, he had already known what we would become. He created us with greatness, made us kings and queens, and gave us dominion over power.

Who God says you are is far from ordinary. All he has written concerning you is dripped in greatness. You are full of potential and there is nothing that can limit how far you will go in the place of destiny. He has destined you to become great and through you, many nations will be fed. You have to give up the thought process that you know what is best because God lets us know that his thoughts are not our thoughts.

> *"For my thoughts are not your thoughts, neither are your ways my ways, says the Lord."*
>
> *-Isaiah 55:8*

What he has in stock for your destiny is beyond what your human understanding could comprehend. He's a great God, and whatever he does also become great. If he declares he has a better plan for your life please know that he means it. However, it's your responsibility to accept it by faith. His plans at times may look so ridiculous but if you can be patient enough to look through it and see beyond what your ordinary eyes can see, you will be able to enjoy your life to the fullest.

He's a God who has never and will never fail. He didn't fail you during creation and he won't fail you in becoming a better person. God says you are the light of the world, a royal priesthood, a holy nation. He calls you nations because he knew you were peculiar and separated apart from the rest. God needs for you to manifest your gift because there are many who can find comfort through you, many who can be saved through you, and many who can be blessed through your generosity. Just for a moment stop believing in coincidence and believe that God was working through me today to remind you to stay focused on him. Imagine that this journal journey is all part of his marvelous plan.

It is your time to shine, so shine your light bright for the world to see. Now is the right time to start believing in yourself, and the things you are capable of doing. Now is the opportune time to take a risk on yourself and chase after your dreams. The Lord said that he is not man that he should lie, and he will grant you the desires of your heart. Our lives are precious in his sight, and when his words enter into your life, they will change the way you think and will allow you to realize that your life is a blessing.

To complete day 1 I want you to ask yourself, who does God say you are? Once you have answered it, believe every bit of it!! If you don't limit yourself, nothing created by God can limit you. Stand on your position today and take what belongs to you through God. You are who God says you are!

## -You Are Created

## *Notes*

Empowered individuals do not concern themselves with the opinions of others. Who does God say that you are? (Although this is the first question, you may not be able to answer this until the end).

_____
_____
_____
_____
_____
_____
_____
_____
_____
_____
_____
_____
_____
_____
_____
_____

## Day 2: Be Awakened

> *"And that, knowing the time, that now [it is] high time to awake out of sleep: for now [is] our salvation nearer than when we believed."*
>
> **-Romans 13:11**

Today's devotional will be about awakening the spirit man lying dormant inside. Have you ever had the feeling as though reality wasn't really reality? Like you are just stuck in a trans doing the same thing day in and day out? The truth is that you have been sleeping in the slumber of the world. This worldly sleep is detrimental because it sneaks up on you, and convinces you that it is your reality. The enemy prefers for you to remain resting in the worldly image of death. If you were truly spiritually awakened you would possess enough to overtake the enemy and his lies of deception in your life. Let me tell you today, the major key to starting a fresh, motivated, and fulfilled day is to answer the awakening call from God through your spirit man. We are living in a generation of cold individuals complacent with comfort zones, who seek to indulge in the endless supply of sleeping pills that the enemy provides.

From the beginning, God has given us the capability to utilize our awakened spirit. He grants us this ability for us to be able to see his plan and to reveal our purpose in life. If you are awakened, you will see what God has in store for your life. God stresses for us to rise up from our slumber and wake up to his call of glorious destiny. This is why studying the work and walking with God every day of your life is essential for your spiritual growth. Are you up for the next level of your life?

> *"Wherefore he says, awake you that sleepest, and rise from the dead, and Christ shall give you light. 15, See then that you walk circumspectly, not as fools, but as wise, 16, redeeming the time because the days are full of evil."*
>
> **-Ephesians 5:15-16**

This scripture is a declaration for our spirit man to rise up from his slumber. There is a great work to be done in you. To lay and rest is to lay amongst the dead. We have got to stop taking our social media sleeping pills and start waking up and living life. We have got to wake up if we aim to align ourselves with the purpose of God. He says you've slept too long and the time for you to rise is now. Those who remain sleeping do so in darkness and are counted as fools. He confirms that once you have awakened that Christ will give you light. A light so bright that no one else will be able to diminish. This light will help to illuminate the lives of others around you. God did not create you to live a self-centered life. You were created to live purposeful and impacting life.

It is foolish to desire to sleep your life away, and still, desire to inherit the riches of the world and a kingdom in heaven. Only a fool would believe that there are no consequences for a life spent in a state of eternal. Consider this your wake-up call. Chose today to awaken your spirit and live amongst the wise or chose to lay in slumber with the dead.

God warned that the days are full of evil, and one of the major evils of your present-day is wasting your time. Don't allow yourself to become caught up in things that are merely a waste of your time. Whether this is people, activities, circumstances, or habits, do not indulge in something that is not contributing to your advancement. When you continue to sleep you will continue to waste your time. Empowered individuals don't allow you to waste their time because it is the one thing you can never give back to them. Likewise, you must adopt this same mentality if you desire to transform your mindset.

If you are not satisfied with the life you are living and you feel as though you have been placed on a repeat cycle of mundane mentality daily, respond to the call to awaken from your spiritual slumber through today's devotion. You need to realize that the devil is trying his best to make you feel as though you can't do what God is calling you to do. The enemy is whispering attacks of limitations in your ears and praying (yes, the enemy prays and preys) that he can continue to convince you that you can't rise beyond your current moment. He wants you to feel useless and be irrelevant. To feel discarded and isolated. He wants you to feel how he feels. He wants you to be reformed in his image. It is up to you to stop listening to the voice that keeps limiting your capability. It is up to you to break away from the comforts of your routine and grow comfortable with becoming uncomfortable. Rise up to the call of greatness through Jesus Christ. Rise up to the call knowing that he wants to change your life today. The awakening call of God is upon you and it is your personal choice to embrace it.

He wants the best for you and now is the best time to respond to his faithful call in order for you to advance to your next level. Always keep your mind alert, focus on the things above, and limit the things that are wasting time in your life.

**YOUR FOCUS POINTS:**

1. **God is always available to me.** You need to focus your mind on the fact that he's forever available to you and he is ready to assist you in all your issues. He is God, he knows all about your storms as well as the desired ending of your journey.
2. **Be positive to his call.** When he says yes, he means it and responds to the positive side of your problems. When he says you should wake up, he knows it will be to your favor and will help you progress towards your desired outcomes. Therefore, be positive to his call by waking up your spirit man to do a mighty work.
3. **The best you desire will only come through him.** Everything you imagine to be great in life is authored by God. God does not only desire for you to have life, but he desires for you to have it abundantly. He wants to take good care of your life, and allow your true light to shine as promised in his word. Come out today

and get the best of your desire through his grace.

4. **Connect with him in the spirit.** Let your spirit be aligned with God so that he may share His thoughts with you. Remember our thoughts are not his thoughts and we should think spiritually so that our thoughts are protected from the enemy. Disconnect yourself from setbacks and discouragement and move closer to him through his words and prayer. Be spiritually inclined to the awakening call of hope and greatness he wants to offer you.

The love of God concerning your life cannot be quantified. The only limit to what he wants to offer you is your inability to respond to the awakening call of your spirit man through him. You must be willing to help yourself in order for him to help you. Say no to your limitations and your discouragers. Say no to the words of the devil. Condition your mind to the things of God and be alive to fulfill his purpose for your life.

# -You Are Awakened

## *Notes*

What are some things that are wasting your time and limiting you from answering your awakening?

_____
_____
_____
_____
_____
_____
_____
_____
_____
_____
_____
_____
_____
_____
_____
_____
_____

## Day 3: Limitless

Today's devotional will be about learning to operate without limits. The way we think can affect the way we make decisions about our lives. If you want to excel in life you must learn to stop limiting yourself. You need to stop believing or even entertaining what limiters have to say about you. Especially when their intentions are to reduce the amount of success you are capable of achieving in life. If you are positive in your decision to serve limitless God, be positive that he did not create you with limits.

**What are limitations?**

Limitations can be rules or even decisions that prevent us from growing or expanding beyond certain positions. Limitations are barriers to fulfilling a promised destiny. Society teaches you that you are absolutely fantastic as long as you operate within your limits. That's the idea of people who are suffering from the stronghold of limitations. They have become convinced that anything out of their comfort zone or their view, isn't obtainable for them. They have become conditioned to thinking small and operate with minimal imagination. Their rigid frame mentality keeps them in a constant state of fear. They are always afraid to try something new or different because the gloom of failure lingers in the back of their minds. These are individuals who love to play it safe and believe that the only way to avoid issues is to do everything that you can to prevent them. This is not the thought process of an empowered individual.

Of course, we all are familiar with the feeling of doubt, feeling frustrated and discouraged when our ideas haven't taken off the way we feel they should have. It is imperative to recognize that this is still a spiritual attack. It is okay to doubt yourself every now and then, but when this is a constant state of mind, it may be an indication that you need to reframe your thought process. Staying in the limited mind set can be energy-sapping and leave you feeling as though you are in a hopeless situation. That is exactly where the enemy wants you, hopeless!!

Remember we are trying to evolve our mindset to see ourselves and our situations through God's perspective. The only way that we can do this is to study his word. You serve a huge God, so it is okay to have huge dreams and ambitions. Everyone in this world is facing a perceived limitation of some sort, but if we would lean on God's word, you will find out that he has already equipped you with the necessary tools to overcome your limitation. Commitment, determination, and dedication can help you to push through your barriers but consistency will help you break barriers. You need to make your dream big enough so that it will influence others around you and silence those who doubt you.

> "1 And Jesus entered and passed through Jericho. 2 And, behold, there was a man named Zacchaeus, which was the chief among the publicans, and he was rich. 3 And he sought to see Jesus who he was; and could not for the press, because he was little of stature. 4 And he ran before, and climbed up into a sycomore tree to see him: for he was to pass that way. 5 And when Jesus came to the place, he looked up, and saw him, and said unto him, Zacchaeus, make haste, and come down; for to day I must abide at thy

> *house. 6And he made haste, and came down, and received him joyfully"*
>
> **-Luke 19:1-6**

This scripture gives us insight into a rich man named Zacchaeus. Zacchaeus desired to see Jesus in an effort to get his problems resolved. He decided that he would seek Jesus when he heard he would be passing by. Immediately Zacchaeus was faced with a serious limitation because of his small stature. With the huge crowd wanting to see Jesus too, he knew there was a potential for him to either have no view or a limited view. This is a situation where many would have thrown in the towel and turned back home, but Zacchaeus was resolutely determined to see Jesus. He refused to be limited or discouraged, because of his stature. He was not as concerned with the crowd and barriers as he was concerned with his goal to meet Jesus. He had the mindset of a barrier breaker. He was thinking like a champion, someone who would be victorious. He was thinking the way God designed him to think. He knew that the only way he was going to fail his mission is if he gave up on the mission. This is how you say NO to limitations.

Your limitation maybe your height, finances, gender, age, race, education, or addiction, etc. Regardless, you have to deal with the right mindset. The mindset of someone who isn't bound by limits. Challenges and barriers will always arise, and when they do, you need to be prepared to respond to them. Don't be afraid to encounter them, they will not break you. They are necessary factors meant to push you forward in taking your place among the limitless. This is you building the mindset and mentality of a champion. This is the mindset of self-made millionaires, and it is truly how people at the top think. Now that you know the secret of giants, we can start mining for some of your inner gold.

What is it that has been limiting your progress in the place of your greatness? Is it your physical ailment like the rich man in Luke 19:1-6? Could it be your family background or poverty? Could it be your lack of education or health issues? God is saying to you today that it is time to stop operating in limitations. It is time to stop exercising your gift within limitations. I need you to be motivated and stand on your position to see what

God is saying concerning your elevation. God knows your situation, and he's still in the blessing business. Rest assured in his grace and he will help you overcome those limitations.

Today your goal is to declare that you have the determination of Zacchaeus to see Jesus. Don't be afraid to think and dream big. Don't be afraid to trust God to move abundantly in your life.

## -You Are Limitless

## *Notes*

What is currently limiting you, and what are you willing to overcome this limitation?

_____
_____
_____
_____
_____
_____
_____
_____
_____
_____
_____
_____
_____
_____
_____
_____
_____
_____

# Day 4: Goal Getter ~Focus On The Prize

> *"I can do all things through Christ who strengtheneth me."*
>
> **-Philippians 4:13**

Today we are going to focus on getting you to identify your goals, and identify what it is going to take for you to achieve those goals. Today we are going to help you become a goal getter! Through God, you can do anything you put your mind into. Your relentless effort to continue pushing will eventually allow you to make it to your desired end. All you have to do is keep your eyes on the prize and focus on what it will take you achieve your goal. People who feel empowered have a clear desired outcome and they are focused on making sure that they do what needs to be done to achieve their desires. You have to be able to keep your pride, fear, and distractions under subjection in order to focus on your goals. This is a goal-getter. A goal getter sets their goals and they do all they can to achieve them. This is what you need to get your goal in life. You need to focus on the prize ahead. You need to ignore the pains and put more concern on the result.

In 1Peter 1:3-5, the bible says, "Blessed be to the God and the Father of our Lord Jesus Christ, which according to his abundant mercy have begotten us again unto a lively hope by the resurrection of Jesus Christ from the dead, To an inheritance incorruptible, and undefiled, and that fades not away, reserved in heaven for you, Who are kept by the power of God through faith unto salvation ready to be revealed in the last time."

Peter's words of encouragement to us here is to keep focus on the finished work of Christ on the cross. God has given us hope through Christ and the readiness to get whatever we've put our minds at. The hope you have in Christ is enough for you to journey through to your promise land. The grace of God is sufficient for you to keep your focus on the things you want to achieve.

Matthew 6:6 says, "But when you pray, enter into your closet and when you have shut your door, pray to your Father who is in secret; and your Father who sees in secret will reward you openly."

I want you to believe this, anything you focus on will eventually be yours with the same mindset you put into it. Being focus can make your heart to be lifted. At the same time, when you are focusing your attention on the wrong thing, you may be discouraged. This is why you need to be more careful about what you focus your attention on. The only positive way to respond to the activities of success is to table your desire to God in prayer. It's the best way to approach focus and goal getting. Pray as if you won't pray. Pray as if tomorrow won't come. Pray as if you need the result now. Prayer is powerful. Prayers show God that we recognize we are incapable without him. It shows to him that we need his help, and if you aren't careful, you will soon get distracted.

The relationship between our hearts, and the things we focus our attention on, is very crucial. If you are the type that always focus on problems, regrets, fear, and pain, you will surely get a result but it may be something that breaks you completely. Your focus is your direction. Your direction leads you to your goal. If you are positive-minded with things you focus your mind on, you will surely get the good result you are looking for. However, if it's the other way around, you won't be shocked to feel your result. I want you to know that there's a great connection between your heart and the things you put your mind on.

It is common for us today to switch to prayer only when we've lost everything and become shattered. However, this is not God aligned and he desires for us to view it differently. He wants prayer to be our first weapon to tackling our problems.

> *"We tend to use prayer as a last resort, but God wants it to be our first line of defense."*
> **-Oswald Chambers**

It's a common tradition we only choose to pray when there's nothing else again working. When hope is completely lost. We pray when we're at the tightest corner of our problems. This is why we are getting things wrong and we're not seeing the kind of result we expect to see. Prayer is the only weapon to fight for success. It's an activity of the secret that brings a man to limelight.

I want you to put aside any form of distraction and focus on God who can make your dreams come through. God will help you achieve anything you want in life. You need to seek him in prayer and keep focusing on the things that help you get the best result you are looking for.

- Get your goal set up.
- Put aside any form of distraction.
- Eliminate fear and push away anxiety.
- Set your time to cry to God in prayer.
- Study the word of God
- Live a life of hope. Keep believing in yourself and your dream.

# -You Are A Goal Getter

## *Notes*

What are some things that are wasting your time, and limiting you from answering your awakening?

## DAY 5: INTERESTED

> *"Seest thou a man diligent in his business? he shall stand before kings; he shall not stand before mean men."*
>
> **- Proverb 22:29**

Today's devotional will be about choosing to take interest in the things that are important to you. The most important things in your life requires commitment, dedication, courage, trust, consistency, discipline, and surely the grace of God. When is the last time that you stopped to question what you were interested in doing? Honestly, what do you enjoy doing? Is there a way to get paid for what you enjoy doing? What interests you at church, your job, your children's school? How can you go about pursuing what interests you? These are the questions of an empowered person.

Reflect on all the prominent individuals you have learned about through history and start questioning what lead them to their actions. I assure you; they did not always feel they were destined to be great. Rather they chose to go after what they wanted; they chose to become interested in the things they found essential to them. Things that were powerful and likely seemed unrealistic to the ordinary eye.

The above bible verse is reminding us of how great we truly are and that we stand before Kings, not just your everyday men. Kings are chosen to lead and rule over their entire kingdoms. They are usually leaders because people believe they are capable and equipped to provide for and oversee the kingdom. Some may be kings from winning a war with a rival and were deemed the conqueror. Kings were revered as someone to aspire to. They were often known to be great and inspirational motivators. It is these characteristics that will stand in front of the elite.

According to Proverb 22:29, Anybody can become a king regardless of his/her background, financial status, and popularity in most cases. Kings are made due to their qualities and abilities. If you can change the way you think, you can change your status. God was declaring that if you were stationed in your assignment you will be stationed in the presence of kings. If you can focus on the fundament things in life, the things that pique your interest, even the sky won't be your limit. If you can learn to say no to the things that won't help you grow in life, you will begin embarking on a journey of becoming the best you. For not only you but for the people around you as well. Kings do not have the time to dwell on their past decisions because they know that there are plenty of future decisions that they will have to make. They know that there are people who are relying on them. In the presence of Kinds, you have to be focused on fundament things about life.

When you are interested in the fundamentals you will become a person who can break limits to cover grounds. People will seek you out for advice because you do not focus on the problem. Rather you focus on the solution. When you have this mindset, you will be respected and valued because you are consciously choosing to be set apart and to be different. Now is the time to choose to focus on what is important in your life. Forget the things of old. Say no to the things that limit your progression and focus on the fundamentals. The things that will encourage you to keep fighting, to keep progressing, and to press towards the mark. I don't care if it is your children, your spouse, your friends and family, business, traveling, or reading, choose to indulge in the pleasures of your interested fundamentals.

God wants you to do something monumental in your life and he is telling you that you need to change the way you think. You need to start focusing on the most important things in your life today because tomorrow is not guaranteed. Focus your attention on things that will help you grow, things that will uplift your spirit and bring out the best in you. Take note that commitment and diligence must be embedded in your thought process in order to truly change your mindset. You need to be aware that it takes these two key factors to transition into a renewed mindset.

> *"He becometh poor that dealeth with a slack hand: but the hand of the diligent maketh rich."*
>
> **-Proverb 10:4**

Changing your mindset is not going to be an overnight process, in fact, it is actually a gradual process. Which is why we are taking this day by day. The important thing is that you have to be willing to work for your desires. This scripture is telling us that we will be poor if we deal with a slack hand. The scripture is not just talking about financially, but spiritually as well. God did not declare in his word that you had to be the smartest, the strongest, or the most recognized to be rich. God said that all you needed to do was be diligent.

Yesterday we focused on being a goal-getter, but today I want your thought process to begin transitioning into becoming a goal setter. I want you to set time aside to actively participate in the things that you are interested in. Pick up a new hobby, visit a new place, or try something you have always wanted to. Discovering new things, you enjoy, or even getting back to things you previously enjoyed, helps you feel more confident in your decision making. Choose to do something that will not only make a difference in your present life but something that will help others as well. Volunteer your time at a place that brings you joy. Keep your watch active, keep pushing, keep being optimistic, keep being interested and engaged. Keep your focus on the fundamental things.

## -You Are Interested

## *Notes*

What are some current things that interest you? How do you propose to make more time to do the things that interest you?

_____
_____
_____
_____
_____
_____
_____
_____
_____
_____
_____
_____
_____
_____
_____
_____
_____
_____

## Day 7: Be Consistent

> *"But they that wait upon the Lord shall renew their strength; they shall mount up with wings as eagles; they shall run, and not be weary; and they shall walk, and not faint."*
>
> - Isaiah 40: 31

Today's devotional will be about breaking away from the "keeping up with the Jones's" mentality and learning to pace yourself with your desires. The beginning of success is always the hardest due to several trial and error attempts, which can often lead to discouragement. For instance, when working out, it is often the most painful and the most challenging in the beginning. The muscles in your body struggle to adjust in the recent burst inactivity and it will oftentimes leave you very sore, and also leave you thinking "why am I torturing myself this way?" Recovery from an initial workout tends to be one of the most discouraging moments for our bodies because it struggles to cope with the expansivity of the body muscles and aches. For some of us, this pain will be enough to make us discontinue the workouts, and embrace the mentality of I am fine just the way I am. We learn to embrace this not because it was our desired outcome, but because we are afraid to subdue ourselves to more pain. Or at least I know this has been my outlook. I have never been a person who was big on working out, in fact, I pretty much avoid it at all costs. My husband, who was (and if you ask him, he will say still is) an athlete, and his outlook on workout pain is very different from mine. When my husband thinks about pain when working out, he associates it with what comes after the pain. He knew that the pain would ultimately lead to gain. Individuals who can see the end product in their minds while going through, are exercising their faith to trust God to give them an expected end. The beginning may look serious and tough, and it may even hurt but you cannot lose focus. You must learn to keep your pace.

Pacing yourself is a key way to overcoming any obstacle. I once had a director ask me, "How do you eat an elephant?" To which he answered, one bite at a time. Trying to overcome your obstacle, situation, or circumstance all at once is usually one of the reasons people give in so quickly. I tell people I minister to all the time, that if it took time for you to get into that situation, it will take even more time to get you out of that situation. You have to gain consistency. It is easy to start something but it is challenging to continue doing something.

Consistency will help you identify just how determined you are to change your circumstances. Once you activate your prayer line with God, you have to be consistent to see an elevation change. Put it like this, are you trying to get fed? or Are you trying to learn how to hunt for food? Do you want to eat for a night? or Do you want to be able to eat for a lifetime? Gaining consistency will bring about skill sets that you did not know you had. Take trying out for a sport that you love, you have to be consistent with practicing to harness your skills. You must have a consistent prayer life to change your dynamics. This is what today's scripture is discussing. Those who are consistent with the lord will have a renewed strength. When we maintain our pace in God, we maintain our standard, allowing life to become less complicated and more effortless.

Anything you continue doing on a regular basis will eventually become a habit. It will become part of your everyday life so much so that if you skip it, it will become foreign for you not to do it. Starting your journey with God will help you build a sturdy foundation and the courage you need to stand out in your uniqueness. His presence will make you take away your concern for any difficulties you are going through.

Like prayer, you have to grow a consistency with reading your bible. So many of us go through periods of despair and seek a sign from God. We claim we desire to hear a word from Him, yet refuse to open our bibles. How can God give you a word if you refuse to go to the source of the word? God wants you to turn your thoughts towards Him so He can give you guidance on your purpose. With God, all things are possible and your relentless effort in pushing forward will be greatly rewarded in the end.

Once you gain consistency it will be easy for you to say no to anything that limits or hinders you in any way. You will be able to say no to any of your discouragers. You will be able to say no to defeat and frustration. Your consistency will keep you from hiding yourself, from hiding the real you. Connect to God and focus on things that will motivate you to move forward and empower you. Hold on to God in anything you are doing because he's the only one who can supply you with exactly what you need. He can encourage you not to give up when you are facing your darkest moments. My prayer is that today you learn that you do not have to fix everything in your life at one time, take it day by day. I want you to identify one area in life your life you would like to improve and begin praying on it today. I want you to consistently pray for it twice a day for the remainder of our journey. I encourage you to pick a time that you know you will be able to remain consistent with and remember the devotional only works if you actually try it. In order for God to renew your strength, you must be consistent.

## -You Are Consistent

## *Notes*

What one area would you improve in your life? How would you go about improving it, how long would it take you to achieve this?

## Day 8: Purposed Prayer

> *"And Jesus said unto them, Because of your unbelief: for verily I say unto you, If ye have faith as a grain of mustard seed, ye shall say unto this mountain, Remove hence to yonder place; and it shall remove; and nothing shall be impossible unto you."*
>
> **- Matthew 17:20**

Today's devotional will be about shifting into purposeful and powerful prayer. The God we serve is a great and miracle-working God. A God who makes the impossible, possible. When was the last time you asked God to do something impossible for you? According to Matthew 17:20, what God requires from us is a little faith mixed with an understanding of who He is. Prayer is the only key that unlocks the treasures of heaven. It's the impulse heaven responses to. When you sing praises to God and make your petition known to Him, He moves on your behalf.

Our text said that if you have faith the size of a mustard seed, you will be able to move mountains. I would like to offer this disclaimer; you cannot exercise this kind of faith if you do not know Him personally. It simply just won't work. Think about it this way, how much faith would you have in a total stranger to pay your rent? We must utilize this same sense when we think about our relationship with God. When you don't really know Him, you don't really have the trust that He is going to do just what He said He would do. The more you build a relationship with Him, and you see He has shown up right on time, every time, you will trust Him. Prayer is necessary for us to get to know God and for us to be able to trust God. Nowadays, I feel that it is so easy for people to lose faith in God because they never truly had faith in Him to begin with. Your faith will be stagnant if you do not keep open communication with Him. The same way communication is essential for any functioning relationship (work, school, family, friends, church), it is even more essential to keep healthy communication with God. It's vital for you to make prayer and fellowship a part of your daily routine.

Sometimes we can be discouraged from praying because we feel as though God knows everything we are going through. So why hasn't he helped? Even though God knows exactly what you are going through, God will keep still because he has given us a power of choice and we have to choose Him. He will show us signs that He sees what we are going through and hints that He is still in the blessing business, but his word tells us that we must ask to receive. Where I grew up there was an old saying "closed mouths don't get fed," meaning if you wanted something, you better ask for it. God has a blessing with your name on it and what He has for you, is for you, you just have to be willing to ask.

When dealing with prayer, we have to make sure that we cast out our past and our pride. These are the two largest hindrances people have expressed to me about prayer. Your past will make you feel as though you are unworthy to seek out your blessings from God. Everyone has a past, and everyone has fallen short, but thanks to the grace of God, we are all still able to have access to the throne. Never let the enemy convince you that you are somehow undeserving to talk to the father. We have got to make sure that we cast out pride. Pride will convince you that you do not need the Lords help. It will have you thinking that you have made it this far without him, so why do you need to bother him now. Pride will make you take your focus away from the enemy who is attacking you, to the people he is utilizing to attack you.

One of the most eye-opening events in my life happened 2 years ago when my son Tye was in the second grade. A few weeks before school ended, I received a call from Tye's teacher that he had been involved in an incident for roughhousing with a little girl. For anyone who knows Tye, he is non-confrontational and he has never been in trouble at school. Everyone was fine, but as a formality, the teacher had to inform me of the incident. I informed Tye his teacher told me the altercation was with a young girl, and he said yes. He informed me the little girl had been instructing two boys to attack him. When I asked him why didn't he tell the teacher? he informed me it was because they were playing. Then after thinking, I asked why he decided to roughhouse with the girl and not the two boys? He said "the boys are my friends and they were following her instructions. She had already sent them to attack me twice, there was not going to be a 3rd attack." Tye learned a lesson in keeping his hands to himself even playing, but I learned a valuable lesson as well. Too often we fall into the enemy's trap of deception, and do not target the enemy at the source, him! Keeping an open line of communication with God will remind you to keep your eye on the enemy, and not the attack. This is why we have to adopt an active prayer life in order to discern the spiritual attacks of the enemy.

A prayer that moves God is a prayer covered in faith. A prayer with genuine intent and understanding. He responses to it even before you end it. When you believe He is able to meet your needs, He will respond according to your belief. He said anyone who will come unto Him must believe that He is able to do exceedingly great things far above what we think or we could imagine. I'm challenging you today to have faith in God and put all your trust in Him because He's the only one who can truly supply you with what you need. He has never failed. You need to know that He's a reward to those who diligently seek him.

When you pray, who benefits from your prayer? Is it you, your family, your church, your friends, who ultimately reaps the reward? When you pray, what is the purpose of your prayer? Is it to change just today, or is it to change generations to come? Are you requesting to eat off of the harvest, or to eat off of the abundance? When you pray for increase, are you praying for a house, or for houses? Our God is not a mediocre God, and therefore does not deserve mediocre prayers. We serve a mighty God, so he deserves mighty prayers. His desire is that we would possess the power to move mountains, not just request the endurance to climb them. When we start tapping into purposeful prayer, we will begin unlocking powerful prayer, and that is something the enemy does not want you to be aware of.

My prayer for you today is that you shift your prayer from the natural to supernatural. From practical to powerful. From accidental prayer to purposed prayer. We have to stop only seeking to pray to God when we are going through our storms in our situations. We must seek to hear a word from Him, even when things are going well. The enemy should be frightened when he feels you pray. There should be a change in the atmosphere. My prayer for you today is that you are able to move a mountain in your life. What is a mountain you could change in your life right now? Something that could break generational curses? What is a purposed prayer for you?

## -You Are Purposed.

## *Notes*

What mountain do you wish to move in your life?

## Day 9: Become Thirsty

> *"This book of the law shall not depart out of thy mouth; but thou shalt meditate therein day and night, that thou mayest observe to do according to all that is written therein: for then thou shalt make thy way prosperous, and then thou shalt have good success."*
>
> **-Joshua 1:8**

Today's devotional will be about creating a thirst for the word of God. Being friendly to the word of God allows you to easily connect with him. God gives reverence to believers who are capable of addressing Him by his word. There is nothing that makes me give my kids the side eye more than when they remind me of a promise, I made to them or when they use my own words against me. It is the same with God. It is much easier to plead our case when we know our promises. You have to make the word part of your daily guild.

Our scripture lets us know that we must meditate on the word day and night. God told us by doing this, we would have "good" success. This is the value God places on his word. God is not man that He should lie, so anything He says in his word; He will surely do. We have got to become thirsty for the word, and it has to be a thirst that only the word can quench. When you are thirsty for the word, you will seek it out day and night. You will recognize that is essential for you to have the strength to make it through the day.

The word of God is powerful and it is a weapon to be used against the enemy. The enemy does not want you to be aware of your weapon because it is stronger than any two-edge sword man could possess. When you shift into having a purposed prayer, you will also access the blueprint to operate the weapon you have in your possession, and the enemy's goal is to have you weaponless. Think about it, if you had to fight someone, would you want to fight someone who is armed or someone unarmed? Now, let's take that a step further, would you rather fight someone unarmed, and does not know how to handle their weapon, or someone who is armed and has been going to the shooting range, all day every day twice a day? God has given you a weapon, it is up to you to learn how to use it. When you keep this weapon with you at all times, the world will not only fight with you, but for you.

Think about the true power in his word. It was the same word He used to create everything He created in the beginning.

> *"In the beginning was the word, and the word was with God, and word was God. The same was in the beginning with God. All things were made by him; and without him was not anything made that was made."*
>
> **-John 1:1-3**

This should tell you that the word is of God himself. Your communication with God becomes more connected when you make His word your guild. Everything, including those who seek to destroy us, was created by God. Thus, He knows their limitations as well. If you want to make progress in life, you need to know God through his word. Spend more time studying the word and connecting your spirit to the throne. The amount of God's word in you shows how strong you are to fight the enemies. When the word is not in you, enemies feel as though they have permission to toil with your destiny. They will bring about all sorts of problems and difficulties so in an effort to discourage you from pursuing your goals in life. It is up to you to decide if they will prevail. The word is meant to guide us and be a lamp to our path. It is meant to allow you to hear the word of God. Too often we seek to hear a word from God, while simultaneously refusing to go to the word. We will state how God's word doesn't work when we haven't even taken the time to study his word to apply it correctly. This would be no different than saying your bicycle is broken because you aren't pedaling. You have to be willing to apply the work to yield the fruit. The amount of God's word in you, helps you to discover yourself. When you're lost in the journey of life, the word helps you to find your path and leads you towards a successful destination. The deeper you dive into it, the clearer your understanding of it becomes.

My prayer is for you to become thirsty! I want you to be empowered through today's devotion so you are one step closer to taking your rightful place in God's kingdom through exercising your gifts. I am going to challenge you to set aside time to study the word every day, twice a day. My goal is for you to spend 5 minutes during the day and 5 minutes at night reading the work. Preferably the same time each day so it will become a habit for you. We are given twenty-four hours in a day, more than enough to fulfill our daily goal. I am only asking you to give God ten minutes of your time each day for the remainder of the devotional. Remember, you are only going to get out of this what you are willing to put in. If the word could work for someone like me, I know the word is capable of doing exceptional things in your life. If you would only thirst for it. The word found me when I was lost, and enlightened me when I was confused. My prayer is that it is now your turn to be blessed. Become thirsty!

## -You Are Thirsty

## *Notes*

Pick two times of day you will read and study God's word? Will you choose to read out of one book or let the spirit guide you daily?

_____
_____
_____
_____
_____
_____
_____
_____
_____
_____
_____
_____
_____
_____
_____
_____
_____

## Day 10: Wonderful Giving

> *"Give, and it shall be given unto you; good measure, pressed down, and shaken together, and running over, shall men give into your bosom. For with the same measure that ye mete withal it shall be measured to you again."*
>
> **-Luke 6:38**

Today's devotional will be about being a blessing to others through giving. The law of giving is simple, yet we fail to achieve it daily because we miss the fact that our blessings are tied to our giving. When you give to others, you prepare yourself to receive. Giving is very crucial in order for you to make progress in life when it comes to receiving blessings. When you give, you command the blessings of God to come into your life. The measure of what you give is in accordance with what you will receive which is why God loves a cheerful giver. If you give with recement, you will be blessed with resentment.

When you begin to understand you have been charged with giving in order to yield the fruit in your life, giving will become a habit to you. You will actively seek out ways to be a blessing to someone else. There is a reason why we hear "Givers never lack". Giving is a way for God to open doors of opportunity into your life.

If you want a renewed mindset and an everlasting connection to the resources of heaven, you must learn how to give without being forced. You must learn how to bless lives and give to people around you without expecting anything in return. Giving does not have to solely be money. You can give your time or your gifts in ministry to someone. You can even give someone your time of day. Sometimes giving someone an ear to listen, is all they truly desire. We are created in God's image, and the same way he desired to be a blessing to us, is how we should desire to be a blessing to others. I would not be telling you anything that I had not tried or that I did not know to be true.

I have always looked to be a blessing to others. I would literally give a person the shirt off of my back. I remember my parents would tell me that I was never going to be rich, because I was always giving stuff away. For a while I thought they were right until I started realizing that whenever I blessed others and someone came right back around and blessed me. God desires to press down, shake together, and have overrunning blessings in your life. Everyone in one way or the other needs your help. It might be the little things you don't consider as important. The clothes you have abandon may be something that will bring joy to others, but don't make a habit out of only giving things you no longer desire. Give out your best in order to command the windows of heaven to be opened to you.

It is important when giving to others to make sure you aren't doing it because you want others to see you. If this was your intention, God will not reward you because you have already sought out your reward from man. Your act of giving should be tailored and guided by the will of God. We need to make giving something we willingly and naturally do from our hearts. The genuineness of our heart will be greatly blessed in God's presence because again, you are blessed according to the measure of which you gave. For instance, if Person A has $10 and gives a person in need $9, and Person B has $100 and gives a person in need $9, who gave more? Although the exact same amounts were given, person A gave more because they gave 90% of what they had, while person B gave 9% of what they had. This is what it means to be blessed according to your measure.

God shows us He was willing to give us his best, we He gave His only begotten Son to be sacrificed on our behalf. This is how important God felt giving should be in our life. He desires to bless you through giving. He desires for you to be of his image and to be a blessing to others. Always give your best and give it with a cheerful heart. Do not give grudgingly. It's a seed of faith, so let it be sowed on fertile ground by giving according to the will of God.

Giving creates an opportunity for you to connect with other people and impact their lives. You may give to someone today and never think twice about it. While the person you are giving to may never forget about it.

My prayer today is that you activate your giving potential. I want you to believe in the power of giving so that all the promises of God concerning your life may be fulfilled. Your ability to give allows you to show your love for others. If you feel as though you have already activated giving in your life, I would like to challenge you to amplify your giving. Become even more of a blessing to someone. Allow God to reveal to you just how blessed you are through helping others. My prayer is that you will become a giver.

## -You Are Giving

## *Notes*

I want to you to find someone to be a blessing to today. I want for you to write down what you did and how it made you feel.

_____
_____
_____
_____
_____
_____
_____
_____
_____
_____
_____
_____
_____
_____
_____
_____
_____
_____

# Day 10: Giving Up Isn't An Option

> *"For I know the thought I think towards you, says the Lord, the thoughts of peace and not of evil, to give you an expected end."*
>
> **- Jeremiah 29:11.**

Today's devotional will be about casting out the spirit of defeat and surrender and embracing the mindset of perseverance. The thing about fear is that it will allow you to feel defeated before you even begin. In this text, God is letting us know that he has placed thoughts toward us. He has a plan towards our life, plans that will give us a bright future. He goes on further to let us know that he has appointed an expected end for us. All we need to do is stay on course. Once you have your trust in him, God will bring to past all your desires. He will help you achieve your goals in life. This will only happen when you put your trust in him. When you put your focus on him, it should bring you comfort realizing you won't fail because he is guiding your every step. God's plans are greater than what we ever could have imagined. It is challenging when you do not know the desired outcome that God has for you. This is why we must activate our prayer life in order to be able to discern the direction God is calling us to go to. Prayer is vital in achieving a renewed mindset.

> *"Be ye strong therefore, and let not your hands be weak: for your work shall be rewarded."*
>
> **-2 Chronicles 15: 7**

The Lord informs us that there is a reward promised for all of our labors. We live in a microwave society, where we desire to see instantaneous results for our work. It is imperative to understand that our reward comes from God in his appointed time, not ours. God designed us to be laborers, yet the world has informed us that we should seek the easy way out. Naturally our spirit man and flesh man clash because they desire to do two extremely different things. God wants you to labor because if you work hard to get it, it will be hard to lose. If it was easy to get it, it will be easy to lose. The less that you work, the weaker you will become, and it is for this reason that God declares that we must continuously do his work.

In this journey called life, there will be many times we feel like giving up. When we feel as though we no longer have hope and all is lost. During this season it may feel as though throwing in the towel is the only option, but this couldn't be further from the truth. This is the time when you need to grind harder than you ever have because the enemy feels as though he has got you right where he wants you. You are against the ropes, beaten, bruised, and battered, but you must stand strong. Even when you don't have the energy to swing back, just stand. The only thought on your mind should be, don't give up.

I remember 15 years ago; I was viciously jumped outside of a night club. I have never been a fighter because I don't condone violence unless it is to protect yourself. However, on this particular night, I was attacked over 3 times by over 13 different women. During the final attack, the big brawl, all I could hear was something telling me to put my back against the wall and whatever you do don't fall because if you fall, they will surely try to kill you. I was 18 at the time and later found out that a few of these women who attacked me were in there 30's and 40's. They busted bottles over my face, ripped pieces of my skin off from biting me, and pulled my shrimp earrings through my ear. (at this moment I realized why women take their earrings off before a fight). They had my face looking as though it was written in braille. I remembered the first words my mother said to me when I stumbled into the house bruised and bloodied, "Kierra did you even swing, did you hit anybody." With blood still on my face, I looked at her and smiled and said: "You would be so proud of me, I was knocking girls down left and right." Of course, she thought it was my concussion talking. The fact that I was smiling as though I won had her even more bewildered, but she had no idea how proud I was in that moment. I had chosen to stand and fight to defend myself and when it was at the darkest moment when I couldn't even swing back; when all I could do was shield myself and brace myself for the next round of blows, I stood firm and tall.

When I went to bed that night, I was covered from head to toe in ice. My mother pleaded with me to go to the hospital but I told her no. I needed to feel my healing. That night while sleeping I heard a voice whisper defeat is in the eyes of the beholder and you never felt defeated. I woke up expecting to finally cry from all of the pain I was in. Now that my eyes could open, I expected to cry when I saw my deformed face. To my astonishment, I didn't have a single bruise or knot on my face. Outside of the broken skin on my chest from the bite and my earlobe having a larger hole in it, I came out practically flawless.

I learned a valuable lesson from this and I thank God all the time that I went through it. I learned so much. I learned that I could take a punch, and although sometimes it would hurt, it wouldn't kill me. I learned that life was short, chase your dreams today because tomorrow isn't promised. I learned to stop operating with fear. Having fear and doing everything to be non-confrontational didn't prevent me from having a confrontation. I learned that as long as I have my back against the wall and my God, that no matter how hard the blows come, as long as I don't give up, I will be victorious. It was through this experience that I really became bold for the lord, and I was able to focus on what God had in store for me.

I want you to believe that nothing will change in our lives if we don't encounter difficulties. The growth you are aiming for only takes place during hard times. We discover a lot about ourselves when we are going through our most difficult moments. It is in these times that we not only learn how strong we are, but we gain a better understanding of how to improve ourselves. If you want the best to show up in your life, you need to keep pushing yourself hard, and pushing yourself forward. This is where your inner gold lies. The gold you are looking for will take some mining, some true digging, and labor in order for it to be discovered. Therefore, I want you to keep pushing until you get what God has in store for you.

Tell yourself you can do it; matter of fact, tell yourself you are going to do it, and you are going to come out all the better for it! Tell yourself that you are stronger than your stronghold, that you are wiser than your problem, and that you have more courage than you have fear. Sometimes you need to encourage yourself, so be sure to tell yourself positive things. We spend more time with ourselves than anybody else, so make sure that you are someone worth being around. Be kind to yourself, and always be mindful of what comes out of your mouth. Make sure you are consistent in saying positive things to yourself even when things seem rough and look discouraging. Continue to believe in God, and trust in his unchanging hand, and know he is a present help in your time of need.

The thoughts that God thinks towards you are thoughts of peace and not of evil. He has thoughts to give you an expected end. Today I want you to focus on the things that are making you feel as though you want to give up, and what it will take for you to overthrow those things.

## -You Are Sedulous

## *Notes*

Is there anything that makes you want to give up on life? What advice would you five to your most treasured loved one if they were in your shoes?

---
---
---
---
---
---
---
---
---
---
---
---
---
---
---

# Revived

## Day 11: Positioned In His Presence

> *"How sweet are thy words unto my taste! yea, sweeter than honey to my mouth! Through thy precepts I get understanding: therefore I hate every false way. Thy word is a lamp unto my feet, and a light unto my path.."*
>
> **-Psalm 119: 103-105**

Today's devotional will be about getting ourselves positioned in front of the Lord. You need to be informed about the place you worship, the ministry you attend, and the pastor who teaches you God's words. These are very relevant in your growth and the way you address issues with the word of God. You need to position yourself right so the right words from God's throne will be positioned on your tongue. God is letting us know the teachings you listen to can determine your awareness in God, which is why He tells you to be leery of false prophets. God knew there would be some people who would falsify themselves in His name. There are so many who claim God has called them, so you have to be cautious who you give an ear because not everyone is called.

The major aim of the church is to be a place of refuge and peace. A place where the word of God is taught for the edification of the body of Christ. They are there for your spiritual growth. There are over 2000 different denominations, all focused on what separates them from one another. God is interested in your development. He wants you to be blessed through the teaching of his words. This is why it is vital that you know your man or woman of God. So, you will be able to discern whether they are making an interpretation of God's word or getting a revelation from God's word.

This is why God tells us to seek out his word and to study and show thyself approved. When you receive the word of God rightly, your steps and feet will be positioned in the right direction. You will know the right steps to take when in difficult moments of your life. The words give you understanding when you are confused and hope when you're discouraged. There is power in God's word, for He is the word. It is crucial to make use of the word of God in every step you take in your life. You must allow the light to be a lamp to your path. The word of God strengthens you and opens your eyes to the essence of obedience. Being positioned in God's word helps you to count your blessings and glorify your Father in heaven for the things to come. Anyone who desires to prosper in life must also desire to prosper the word of God as well. You must position yourself in the right place to receive the word of God in order for your mindset to be revived. A pastor should allow the doctrine of the word to be the foundation of their instruction. They are positioned to breakdown and simplify God's message appropriately. Their goal is to help you better understand God and his desire for you. When you are positioned in the right place with God, you will grow in God's wisdom.

Think about it like this, your body was designed for you to talk and walk in an upright position, righteousness. Now think about getting out of the position of righteousness and squatting into the position of unrighteousness. Initially, your weight will be easily sustainable for you to hold up, but the longer you stay in the position that wasn't designed for you, the more pain you will experience. Even though your weight does not change while you are squatting, the burden it places on the body does change. It is the same thing when we hold ourselves out of position with God.

My prayer is that you get back in alignment with God. Today I want you to think about your position in God's presence and about those who bring you the word. Anything you desire to become in life is obtainable through God's word. The word is a special and perfect prerequisite to spiritual elevation. So many of God's children are suffering because they lack the word or they are positioned in the wrong place. They are easily tormented by the enemy because they are out of position with God. Fellowship with true children of God and attend churches that teach the word according to the will and instruction of God. My prayer is that you get back into position with God.

## -You Are Positioned

## *Notes*

Do you feel that you are positioned in God's presence? What steps could you take to get back into the right position with God?

___

## Day 12: Take A Stand

> *"Be strong and of a good courage, fear not, nor be afraid of them: for the Lord thy God, he it is that doth go with thee; he will not fail thee, nor forsake thee."*
>
> **-Deuteronomy 31:6**

Today's devotional will be about making courageous decisions and standing up for the things that you believe in. In decision making, always stay strong and be courageous. When you are consistent in your decision making, you will do well and be guided into better choices. People who stay focused and maintain their stance will find their steps ordered towards success.

When we think about Daniel, it was his courage to stand by his beliefs that led to him being cast into the den of Lions. Daniel trusted God so much he was willing to bet his life on it. This is what it means to stand in agreement with the Lord, regardless of how low-spirited the situation appears to be. One key element most people forget is that Daniel was not in the lion's den alone. He had God with him every step of the way. Just as the Lord did not forsake Daniel, He will not forsake you. In today's society we are taught you are a coward if you do not physically fight someone, but Daniel is a reminder that every battle isn't yours to fight. Sometimes the Lord doesn't need you to fight at all. All he needs for you to do is stand tall. This can be challenging to grasp because naturally when we are under attack, be it social media, work, or wherever, we have the natural tendency to defend ourselves. God lets us know that you don't have to show up to every fight you are invited to. Sometimes all you need to do is just stand.

You need the right mind gifted with the focus of the Lord to be able to stand firm and remain immovable on the things you believe in. It is like the phrase my grandmother told me throughout my entire childhood, "Stand for something, or fall for anything". In order to stand strong, you have to believe in yourself and possess a strong moral ethics compass. You must maintain a high level of integrity and understand the value of self-worth. When you know you stand in God, you will be bold to make the necessary decisions to progress and elevate yourself. Even if it means upsetting others around you. Even when you have a crowd surrounding you, demanding you conform to their ideals. If you stand strong on the word of God, He will ensure you are victorious. You will be confident about the things you want for your life and what needs to go. You will know that God cannot fail. You were created in the image of God, also will not fail.

Put your mind on what it is you desire. Believe it and go for it. Work towards achieving it every day little by little. Believe in yourself and make your own decisions and stand by them. I encourage you today to stand strong and be immovable in whatever God has you enduring. Continue praying and singing praises unto Him while it appears you are down and out. When you stand on the word of the Lord your enemies will be put to shame because every knee must bow. God will never forsake you and is always available to save you from your problems. He is a present help in times of need. He loves you and desires the best for you. He wants you to make your decisions confidently so that you will stand by it until you see your expected end. We should always seek God out prior to making any major decisions in order to avoid making mistakes.

God desires greatness for your life and wants you to see how important your life is to Him. He wants to give you the desire of your heart and bless you beyond your wildest dreams. He wants you to keep your hope in Him and stand strong in everything you do. Our God is omnipresent and He's always with you in any situation, but it is your responsibility to let Him know you trust Him.

My prayer for you today is that you diligently seek the Lord before you make any decisions. I pray that you grow confident in your decision making so that you don't find yourself swaying back and forth in life frequently. I pray that you will be revived and stop contemplating on whether or not to elevate yourself and start deciding its time for elevation. I pray that you stand tall for your belief in the Lord.

## -You Are Standing

## *Notes*

In what areas do you feel you need to stand strong in? How can God help you stand strong?

_____
_____
_____
_____
_____
_____
_____
_____
_____
_____
_____
_____
_____
_____
_____
_____
_____

## DAY 13: BE RIGHTEOUS

> *"For the righteous Lord loveth righteousness; his countenance doth behold the upright."*
>
> **-Psalm 11:7**

Today's devotional will be about getting on the right path with God by renewing your righteousness. Every morning we wake up should be seen as a gift from the Lord, and desire to do His will by aiming to what we know would be pleasing in his eyesight. God desires for us to be righteous so that we are morally justified. He knows the troubles of the world can way you down, which is why he desires for us to operate with a clean conscious. Every night that you can lay your head down saying "I know I did my best today" is a day won! I will not pretend like every day is going to be perfect or that you are going to win every night. Though I will tell you that if you make a conscious decision to live a righteous life daily, you will have more wins than losses.

When you think about getting yourself on the right track with the Lord, you must also think about getting yourself back on the right track with the people around you. The Lord wants you to have peace. As long as you are walking around harboring guilt, pain, or wronging you have caused someone, you will never have peace. When it comes to individuals who have hurt you, realize they were placed in your life to distract and break down the strongest of us. The more you hold on to resentment, the more damaging it becomes for the body. God wants us to get it right and be upright individuals.

God desires for us to get right by letting go of toxic habits and toxic people. Too often we hold on to the very thing that is draining us mentally, spiritually, and financially. We tend to believe the lesson is always in holding on when sometimes the lesson is in letting go. I remember when I was driving on an icy road one day and I began to hydroplane. I started gripping the steering wheel attempting to gain control of the car and it began to sway back and forth. When the passenger in the car yelled "let go" I immediately let go, and the car quickly got back on track. Sometimes God is yelling for us to let go, but we fail to do so because we're afraid of not being in control. He desires that we trust Him. In fact, He wants you to put all your hope in Him. He wants you to trust His will.

Being righteous means you are making an investment in you. By being righteous you invite blessings into your life. Your decree to restrain yourself from the joys of the world in order to receive the joys of the kingdom is one way to let the Lord know you are ready to receive your blessing. We live in a society that teaches you self-indulgence is a must and it is the standard thing to do, but God did not design us to be standard. He said we are a peculiar people. Making the choice to sacrifice is a Christ-like characteristic that only a few choose to possess.

I pray today's devotional brought a word of encouragement to you. I want you to get right, get in order, and get focused on God. Continue trusting God to elevate you to your next level. He wants you to have the right mind like him. Build your trust by believing in Him and by exercising your faith.

My prayer is that today's devotional encourages you to let go of the things that hold you back, and learning to embrace righteousness, even when it looks like sacrifice. Continue to invite blessings into your life by working on improving your relationship with God. I pray you recognize that you have the power to choose righteousness.

## -You Are Righteous

## *Notes*

Are there any toxic areas you need to remove from your life? How would you go about removing them? In what other ways can you get right with the lord?

_____

_____

_____

_____

_____

_____

_____

_____

_____

_____

_____

_____

_____

_____

_____

_____

## Day 14: Walk In Love

> *"I therefore, the prisoner of the Lord, beseech you that you walk worthy of the vocation wherewith you are called. With all lowliness and meekness, with longsuffering, forbearing one another in love; enduring to keep the unity of the spirit in the bond of peace."*
>
> **-Ephesians 4:1-3**

Today's devotional will be about learning to walk in God's love and applying it to our everyday life. God is love! To be created in the image of God is to be created in the image of love. He wants us to show love to everyone around us and walk in love and peace with our neighbors. This is His will for us. If you are filled with the love of God, it will not cause you grief to show love to people around you. It amazes me just how many Christians strife and compete with one another. When all God desires is that we love and support others. We should love on individuals when they are succeeding and being blessed, not just when they are going through difficulties.

When you choose to love people, it is important to understand that love is an action word. It is not something you say, it is something you show. The same way you should never have to question whether or not someone loves you is the same way a person should not have to question whether or not you love them. When you love someone, you love them unconditionally. This means that you have to be accepting of their faults. When you love someone, you aren't fixated on changing them, because you know that if God has not changed them there is no need to change them. If you love a person, you pray for them in their sin, not chastise and curse them for it. When you love others, you exemplify Christ.

God desires for us to live our daily life in pursuit of perfection through loving and caring for others. You don't have to be in a constant good mood to walk in love with others. It is an extraordinary thing to testify to others on how you handled and overcame difficult situations through the grace of God. Loving God's creation identifies to others that you are a true child of God. You resemble someone who has been in the presence of the Father. Someone whose success people are waiting and rooting for.

> *"Charity suffereth long, and is kind; charity envieth not; charity vaunteth not itself, is not puffed up, Doth not behave itself unseemly, seeketh not her own, is not easily provoked, thinketh no evil; Rejoiceth not in iniquity, but rejoiceth in the truth;*
>
> *Beareth all things, believeth all things, hopeth all things, endureth all things. Charity never faileth: but whether there be prophecies, they shall fail; whether there be tongues, they shall cease; whether there be knowledge, it shall vanish away."*
>
> ***1 Corinthians 13:4-8***

It is amazing when you display love how people naturally attract to you. My grandmother is 86 years old, and I am pretty sure that half of San Antonio, Texas calls her grandma. Even when she walks into the store, people hug her and greet her and call her grandma. The reason is because she always treats people with love and kindness. She always welcomes strangers with open arms. Since before I was born my grandmother cooked a large supper every Sunday and she would make sure that not only her family ate, but that the whole neighborhood ate as well. I find myself often saying "love like this doesn't exist anymore." Really the issue is so few of us draw close to his love to know how to reciprocate it. When you give agape love, you will be astonished when others begin to attract to you. Your lifestyle will start to draw men unto God because you are taking joy in doing well to others. You will begin to draw even the least of them. People who could not stand you in high school will desire to be in your presence. You will be truly amazed at just how many people are craving for someone to love them.

To walk peacefully and according to the will of God with others is our calling. His desire is that we are humble, patient, and compassionate to others. Be slow to anger by focusing on the grace of God. Exercise your patience. It has been said that patience is an exhibition of God's activities in us. Wait for His wonders in your life. Wait for it to manifest in your aspirations, in your career, and all the things you want to achieve. He'll make things happen on your behalf. Keep your hope active and lively and He will make you come out strong. More than being patient with others, be patient with yourself. I say it all the time that we are our worst critics. It is going to take time for you to evolve into the person you desire to be. Make sure you take the time to love yourself properly. It is beyond challenging to encourage someone to love you the right way, when you don't know how you like to be loved. Christians, believers, and society in general needs to indulge in the practice of self-love more.

Love is the most principal element of being a Christian. We're called to love our neighbors as we love ourselves. My prayer for you today is that you walk through your day without having negative thoughts of others, and instead look for ways to instill love in them. That co-worker who is driving you up a wall, take a moment to question why she acts the way he or she acts. It doesn't cost us anything to love others and we should be passionate about helping others. My prayer is that your heart is transformed with love. Walk daily in love and see just how beautiful your life is. Embrace the thought of not only giving love to others but also embrace the thought of learning how to receive love. My prayer is if there is anything holding you back from receiving the love of God, or the love from others, that you cast it out and allow God to be your safe refuge. Today I want you to focus on how you can love yourself more, and how you can love others more.

## -You Are Love

## *Notes*

What does love look like for you? How do you like to be loved?

## Day 15: Think Big

> *"Finally, brethren, whatsoever things are true, whatsoever things are honest, whatsoever things are just, whatsoever things are pure, whatsoever things are lovely, whatsoever things are of good report; if there be any virtue, and if there be any praise, think on these things."*
>
> **-Philippians 4:8**
>
> *"For as he thinketh in his heart, so is he: Eat and drink, saith he to thee; but his heart is not with thee."*
>
> **-Proverbs 23:7**

Today's devotional will be about embracing the 'think big' notions and casting out doubts that hinder you from pursuing your big plans. Throughout my journey, I have met people with different and extraordinary goals. People who have done great things with humility. In life, it is much easier to achieve success with determination and the love of God. People who dream big dreams and do great things are people who are willing to embrace the thought of being more. More than their current state or situation. More than their past hurt and pain. People who think big are people who have embraced self-love. They have grown to understand that it's okay for them to be great. It's okay for them to chase their dreams. It is okay for them to be in the image of God. These individuals embody and embrace love.

God let us know what our thoughts should be focused to. He gave us a list: think noble, think right, think pure, think lovely, and think praiseworthy, because what you think you are you will be. So many people come to me and ask what made me decide to write and my answer is always the same. "I thought I had a message worth sharing." Once I started believing I could do great things greatness no longer felt like a dream, it felt as though it was my destination. Confidence is necessary for you to transition your mind from thinking day to day thoughts, to legacy thoughts.

People who think big realize they don't fit in. Try as hard as they may, they just cannot seem to find a group or setting they belong to. In fact, they may even gain a reputation of being unrealistic, non-complacent, or a dreamer. I can recall when my husband and I were dating, it would frustrate him that I never seemed to be content with life. Although I was grateful for my life, grateful for my blessings, and just grateful to know God personally, I would have this constant nagging sensation of *greater is on the way*. When you think big, please understand that it is perfectly okay for your dreams to seem unrealistic to people. Think back to the stories in the Bible. Can you imagine a modern-day Noah? Never be afraid to embrace the thought of greatness, as all greatness begins with a thought. To think big, you must know your God intimately. You must know who He is and what He is capable of doing. You must love as He has instructed. You must choose to do good to others and to yourself. You must embrace peace so that you can embrace elevation. You are who you think you are.

One of the key lessons I learned from my years in management, is that a person's perception becomes their reality. When a person believed they worked for a great company, it was a great company for them. When they believed it was a terrible company, it was. The company never changed but the way it was viewed did. How you think is important. So, it is imperative that you have the right mindset. You need to first think you have the capability to do great things, to actually do great things. Possess the power and ability to make things work better for your life by thinking right. You need to have this mindset that you are royalty.

You are a child of the king handcrafted to perfection and an heir to the throne. When you say yes to God, you say yes to all of the riches of heaven. Therefore, think as though you were a King. Think like someone who has authority! Think with courage. Rebuke those who seek to discourage you. Rebuke any forms of anxiety. Declare with authority you are far from discouragement.

My prayer for you today is that you think beyond your normal state of self. Today I want you to begin thinking abnormally, as though you were peculiar. Think as though you weren't afraid because you know you have an expected outcome. Think big as though you were created by God! Remember, what someone thinks in their heart, so they will believe with their mind. My prayer is that you learn to think with your heart.

## -You Are A Thinker

## *Notes*

Think about your ideal career. Now create a vision board of what this career will create in your life (house, car, generational wealth). What steps are needed to make this dream a reality?

_____
_____
_____
_____
_____
_____
_____
_____
_____
_____
_____
_____
_____
_____
_____
_____

## Day 16: Be Disciplined

> *"For God hath not given us the spirit of fear; but of power, and of love, and of a sound mind."*
>
> **-2 Timothy 1:7**

Today's devotional will focus on becoming disciplined to yield the fruits in your life. Discipline is very crucial in every aspect of life. Our flesh desires worldly pleasure and does not desire to stress itself in any form. We cannot always allow our flesh to gain its lustful desires because it will subject you to defeat. If you continue lowering your potentials for self-gratification, you will cease to take action against unworthy desires. Gambling, gluttony, addiction, promiscuity, and so many other areas that lead to a downward spiral, all start with a lack of discipline. To come out of the enemies suppressing power, you must learn to discipline yourself. Discipline is what separates the strong from the weak. Discipline impacts every aspect of your life. Your home, church, school, work, relationships, eating, or obtaining goals. No matter what it is, discipline is essential in achieving it. In renewing your mindset and mining your inner gold, you are going to need to possess self-discipline.

## What is self-discipline?

Self-discipline is the ability to take full control of yourself in order to do what is needed to advance yourself. It is the power that enables you to stick to your decisions and maintain them without compromise. This display of 'willpower' is what separates us from other creatures.

> *"It's the capacity to restrain our impulses, resist temptation in order to do what's right and good in the long run, not what we want to do right now. It's central in fact, to civilization."*
>
> **-Dr. Roy Baumeister *Ph*.D.**

Dr. Roy explains that possessing and exercising discipline will teach you how to restrain your impulses and resist temptation. I have never met an athlete who did not have a disciplined mentality. This is because they know it is necessary in order to achieve their goals. Willpower permits us to choose what we desire, but discipline will aid us to reach our expected end. The enemy wants you to focus on now, but discipline will allow you to focus on the future. The gap between your success and accomplishment is your own self-discipline. If you can't discipline yourself, you won't rise to your full potential. Instead, you will adopt a "common man's" mentality. You will believe that only something that is gratifying to your senses is beneficial to the body, but it is detrimental to the soul. Lack of self-discipline leads to an influx of self- gratification. A disorder that is rapidly on the rise today.

> *"We don't have to be smarter than the rest; we have to be more disciplined than the rest."*
>
> **-Warren Buffett**

Allow this quote to really resonate with you. We often buy into the misconception that we have to be the smartest, the richest, or the most powerful, when really the core is that you must be more disciplined than your competitor. Being smart will not guarantee that you will be successful, but being disciplined will. Your ability to discipline yourself determines the amount of success you acquire. Success is not for lazy people, well at least not long-term success.

Someone who is disciplined is comfortable with a lost and forgotten word, "NO". Utilizing the word, no, will allow you to set boundaries for yourself. It will allow you to cut off whatever will hinder you from advancement. Say no to things that are not pleasing in his eyesight. Say no to self-indulgences that only offer temporary joy. Say no to the conformity of this world, and be released by the renewing of your mindset. Grant yourself power by exercising your discipline. Put your body under sacrificial subjection. Create opportunities for your advancement through diligence, discipline, and consistency. Confront any limitation that stands as a barrier to your progress. Start thinking about what you desire to know what you want to do and focus your mind on them to get the best result you ever desire.

My prayer for you today is that you remember God's spirit is within you. He desires for you to do exceedingly great. Far above what you can think, but it will require discipline for you to see it manifest. Start transforming your thought process on who you are. It doesn't matter if your goal is to lose weight, gain consistency in your household, to get a promotion or a new job. It will require discipline to get there. Today I want you to really focus on how you can better implement discipline into your life to create healthy habits. My prayer is that you increase your discipline in order to attract success!

## -You Are Disciplined

## *Notes*

In what areas of your life could you increase your discipline? List three steps that would help you achieve consistency in these areas?

___
___
___
___
___
___
___
___
___
___
___
___
___
___
___
___
___

## Day 17: Be Fearless

> *"Yea, though I walk through the valley of the shadow of death, I will fear no evil: for thou art with me; thy rod and thy staff they comfort me."*
>
> **-Psalm 23:4**

Today's devotional will be about casting out the spirit of fear to tap into your elevation. If you are a child of God you must begin trusting that you have nothing to worry about. There is no need for you to wallow in fear while going through your struggle. God has already declared you victorious. His rod of defense is available to comfort you when you need it most.

When you are going through your valleys, it can feel as though you are all alone. It can feel as though the shadow of death (spiritual death, financial death, emotional death) may be looming over you. You do not need to be afraid because God says He is with you. Fear is a torment implemented by the enemy. The enemy knows that if he can defeat you before you ever get started, he will always be victorious. It is a strong weapon of the devil. He uses it to oppress his victims. Fear comes when we are lost in the midst of our challenges. It overtakes us when we lose hope. It is used to make us to feel weak and timid. It offers pain and a spirit of hindrance. If you choose to remain in fear you will choose to remain in the bondage of misery.

Be strong and be courageous in whatever it is you choose to do. Say no to fear because when you fear of taking action, nothing reasonable has taken place in your life. These are things you need to drop in order to be in the right place in God. Remember that "FEAR" is a torment; the strong weapon of the devil against the mind. When fear grips you, you lose focus, you lose confidence, you lose total control of yourself. You will begin to respond to the negative words people are saying concerning you. You will become your greatest enemy because you will hate yourself based on others views. This is the reaction and response of our mind from outside stimuli. It will keep hitting us hard if we don't wake up and deal with it.

When you are on the Lord's side, you will respond to things that will make your life useful. When you want to function in the glory of God, you need to stay away from fear because God doesn't respond to anxiety. When his angels visit men the first instruction they give is to "Fear not", because they know what fear can do. They know where fear can allow the mind to go. It is the enemy's tool used to constrain man's capability. God desires for us to operate without fear of the enemy. Christians frequently fall into the attack of fear because they have read scriptures where God requests, they operate with fear.

> *"The fear of the Lord is the beginning of knowledge; fools despise wisdom and instruction."*
>
> **-Proverb 1:7**

In this text, God uses the word fear and he informs us fear is the beginning of knowledge. The fear God talks about in reference is aligned with respect. When you fear the Lord, it shows you respect him. The respect of the Lord is the beginning of knowledge. We have to respect God. When you apply this definition to fear, can you understand why the enemy does not want you to fear the enemy? In this case, fearing the Lord makes life productive and prosperous. It is no different than how our parents put fear into us when we were children. We were conditioned to respect them and their rules. When you fear the Lord, it shows you love Him. It takes wisdom to love and reference the Lord because things that look like unescapable valleys to us, are nothing more than a stepping stone for the Lord.

Don't allow the enemy to use your mind as a place of safe refuge. Don't allow him to use your past against you. Don't allow him to limit your value, your purpose, or your worth through one of his favorite tools. Don't allow yourself to become a slave to fear. Don't fall back into the enemy's same web of entrapment.

My prayer for you today is that you cast out fear that is associated with doubt and failure, and replace it with courage and confidence in your Lord and savior. Fear that is not of God will only lead to regret and shame. It will leave you questioning, why didn't I believe in me more? It won't make you rise beyond the normal level. In fact, it will make your life stagnant. Fear will prevent you from moving forward in life. It will keep reminding you of your inability and faults. It will take time and devoted prayer to remove the enemy's stronghold of fear, but if you are diligent in seeking God you will overcome it. My prayer is that you begin to question your source of fear. One can make life miserable, while the other can make a life abundant. Choose the one you want to exercise in your life.

## -You Are Fearless

## *Notes*

What puts fear in your heart? What are some preventative steps that can help you overcome your fear?

## Day 18: Be Strong

> *"The name of the Lord is a strong tower: the righteous runneth into it, and is safe.."*
>
> **-Proverb 18:10**
>
> *"The righteous cry, and the Lord heareth, and delivereth them out of all their troubles."*
>
> **-Psalm 34:17**

Today's devotional will be about coming out strong in whatever we are going through. Our strength can only be found in God as He is the only one who can help us come out strong in every issue of life. He has promised us great things, and he will surely bring them to pass if only we believe we possess the potential to do so. Fulfillment in a revived mindset can only come into existence if we believe that it will.

Proverbs lets us know that the name, just the name of the Lord, is a strong tower. Meaning all we need to do is simply call on His name. He goes on to say that His name is strong and mighty and that it would be a safe refuge. Being strong does not mean you are the biggest, baddest, or the mightiest. It simply means that you are safe and secure. I remember there was a time I would get so infuriated when I would be misdiagnosed as having SBWC "Strong Black Woman Complex". I would struggle to figure out why people made this determination about me. Was it my job, my appearance, my attitude, my finances? What is it about me that drew the same conclusion from so many? God finally told me; "it is your security." You are not only secure, but you make sure that those who are around you are secure. When you offer a sense of safety and refuge to others, despite all you have endured and despite your setbacks, it shows your strength.

When you cry to God in all your worries, He will help you. According to proverbs 18:10, His name is a strong tower; a complete protection for those who trust in God. The righteous run to Him and they are spared; they hope in Him and they are not ashamed. He will stay with you in times of trouble, and He desires to be your safe refuge. You come out strong when all your hope is in God. You come out strong when you continue to believe in His wonders. He hasn't forgotten you and He will always fulfill any promise He tells you. It is important to understand that coming out strong in a situation is by the grace of God, not your earthly wisdom or knowledge. This is why you have to acknowledge God in everything you do. Putting Him first will make the journey easy for you. This is the secret to coming out strong in that situation.

> *"And we know that all things work together for good to them that love God, to them who are the called according to his purpose.*
>
> **-Romans 8:28**

This is the word of God that we should embed into our hearts. Everything will work to your favor because you have God backing you up. It should bring you strength in your current situation knowing that everything you are experiencing is working together for your good. It is easy to feel like God has forsaken you when you feel as though you are constantly enduring storm after storm, but consider your spiritual strength the same way you would look at your physical strength. In order to build strength, you must be willing to work out and strain your muscles. Expose them to new elements that cause them to stretch further than what they did before. The more you repeat this process, the more muscle memory you build, and the stronger you become. The same holds true for your spiritual strength, the more you get through storms, the more muscle memory you retain, and the less strenuous your storms will become. This will solely be because you have increased your strength.

To increase your strength, you have to be willing to come out of your confined state and live a revived life. A life that inspires transformation in others and has the power to influence generations. There are lives that have been entangled into your life and these individuals are ready for you to fester up the strength to chase your wildest dreams and are looking to you for help in fulfilling their destiny. They are waiting for you to shine your light on them so they too will shine. Don't fail those who are counting on you. Don't think small because you will receive small.

My prayer for you today is that your spirit be endowed with strength. Keep pushing and desire more through Him and hope for a better future.

## -You Are Strong

## *Notes*

Do you think that you are strong? Why or why not? How can your strength be increased?

## Day 19: Being Content

> *"Not that I speak in respect of want: for I have learned, in whatsoever state I am, therewith to be content. I know both how to be abased, and I know how to abound: every where and in all things I am instructed both to be full and to be hungry, both to abound and to suffer need. I can do all things through Christ which strengtheneth me."*
>
> **-Philippians 4:11-13**

Today's devotional will focus on what it means to be content in the world and content in spirit. It is easy to look at your neighbor and decide you deserve their blessings. Your neighbor may make less money and indulge in a life of sin. You may just think you are more deserving, but I beg for you not to convent your neighbor. You have no idea what storms God has placed in their lives, nor do you understand the reasoning why God is blessing them the way He is blessing them. I am frequently told how fortunate and blessed I am and how easy my life looks, to which I always respond,

"I thank God I don't look like what I have been through". It is important that as Christians we learn to stay in our lane. Just because you see a person exercising a gift and it yielding prosperous for them, does not mean you should go out and strive to do the same thing. I am in no way saying that you should not do what successful people are doing, I am merely saying that if you are going to be a copycat, be careful which cat you choose to copy. What God has for you, it is for you, so you need to possess a desire to find what works best for you. Allow God to work in, on, and through you in your quest. Be content with things you have and watch God add unto you. There is nothing worse than letting your plate get cold because you were too busy watching someone else's plate.

As Christians, I don't think contentment is something we place emphasis on. We are constantly being reminded of how we need to do better, sin less, love more, and increase righteousness, so much so that we seldom take the time to appreciate our current state. I mean really take a moment and sit back and thank God for all that He has done thus far. All of his provisions, all of his grace, all of his mercy and forgiveness. I am not saying that we should not set our eyes towards the future. However, I am saying, we should take moments to sit back and appreciate our current state. When you are spiritually content, it prevents you from being bullied into false righteousness. Have you ever gone to a church that made you feel like your apparel was engraved with your sins? They immediately encourage you to become righteous overnight? When you are content in the Lord, you will have no problem reminding Christians that everyone's walk is unique and that you are well equipped on your pressing way.

Doing great things God promised in His word requires understanding, wisdom, being in the right place at the right time, and being disciplined. Even though your current situation may be tough for you, you just have to find a state of contentment. Even if it is knowing that this is not your desired end. You can make this happen through prayer and your commitment to God. He called Abraham and told him to move out of his father's land to a place where He would show him. Indeed, He showed him it was a place full of milk and honey. Abraham became a blessing to his generation because he obeyed God's instructions and follow the directions, He asked him to follow. He was content with what he had and God gave him even more. This is how God will bless your life if you focus on and put all your trust in Him.

My prayer for you today is that you grow content with your current spirituality so that you can tap into a boldness in the Lord. Being content is an attitude, it isn't a state of being. It is the outlook we choose to have in our situation. I pray today's word was uplifting and has encouraged you to take charge of your mindset. I pray that you grow content in salvation.

## -You Are Content

## *Notes*

What does it mean to be content in your eyes? Do you think it is possible to be content in salvation? If so, how?

## Day 20: Fall In Love

> *"Nay, in all these things we are more than conquerors through him that loved us. For I am persuaded, that neither death, nor life, nor angels, nor principalities, nor powers, nor things present, nor things to come, Nor height, nor depth, nor any other creature, shall be able to separate us from the love of God, which is in Christ Jesus our Lord.."*
>
> **-Romans 8: 37-39**

Today's devotional will focus on the significance of falling in love. The will of God for our lives is that we live in love. Our God is love and to truly demonstrate His likeness, we must love ourselves and everyone around us. He said we should love our neighbors the same way we would love ourselves. There is a difference when you love someone and when you are in love with someone. When you are in love with someone you are emotionally connected with them. When you are in love, it borders the line of infatuation. They are constantly on your mind and they are the center of your focus. When you are in love, it is something you are passionate about. This is why we have to fall back in love with Jesus, so we can be passionate about what He has in store for our lives. We need to be in love with His message and His will for our lives. There should be nothing in the world that can separate us from God.

> *"And we know that all things work together for good to them that love God, to them who are the called according to his purpose."*
>
> **-Romans 8:28**

When you want to live an appreciable and fulfilling life, you must show love to others. You need to love who you are, love your personality, as well as love your shortcomings. Embracing love, charity, and goodwill in whatever we do, so we can have positive effects on our lives and the lives of others. Always live to love because God is love!

Make it your everyday habit to live and love. Love what you do and appreciate the outcome of your efforts. When you decide to embark on a journey, make sure it's something you desire. The journey may be your career, your academics, your business and any other aspects of life. Whatever it is, make sure it's something worth spending your time on. When you love what you do and have a desire to do what you are doing, even the thought of failure won't be enough to separate you from your love. Consider Thomas Edison, it is reported that he failed at making the light bulb over 1,000 times before he finally got it right. His love of his work is what kept him persistent in what he was doing. Come rain or shine, you must be determined that nothing will separate you from your love.

Until you love yourself, what you do and the reasons why you are doing them, won't go far in your journey to advancement. In order to see to result, I mean great results, you need to first fall in love with what you are doing.

My prayer for you today is that you move close to your goals with the desire to have a better ending by seeking to fall in love. God goes on further to say that everything you are going through works together for your good, so take a moment to appreciate your current state. Take a moment to love on your children, love on your spouses, and just enjoy that you have made it to another day. God loves you and He wants you to love yourself and what you are currently doing. More importantly, He wants you to fall back in love with Him.

## -You Are In Love

## *Notes*

What are some things that are wasting your time, and limiting you from answering your awakening?

_____
_____
_____
_____
_____
_____
_____
_____
_____
_____
_____
_____
_____
_____
_____
_____

## Day 21: Harvest Time

> *"Say not ye, There are yet four months, and then cometh harvest? behold, I say unto you, Lift up your eyes, and look on the fields; for they are white already to harvest."*
>
> **-John 4:35**

Today we will be closing our 21-Day devotional by focusing on our harvest. Staying consistent, committed, persistent, and disciplined in the Lord has been a focus over the last 21-days, and it has been building you up to yield great results. You have been unknowingly drafting a message to the Lord, letting him know that it is harvest time. If you have followed the steps in this journal, you now have composed a purposeful and powerful prayer. I want you to rip out every notes page (OMG and author advising you to tear apart their work, YES), that's right tear every page out, and make a commitment review your customized prayer. You have been putting in some real work with this journal. You have taken the time to read, taken the time to pray, and taken the time to write.

Every night for 21-days, I want you to read your notes out loud, so you can hear your tailored message to God. This devotional was work and when a man works, it is expected for such a man to reap a harvest. A farmer who has labored in the fields, experiences no greater joy than seeing his harvest. Before you know it, you will be enjoying the fruits of your labor as well.

The harvest time is the time to rejoice. It is a cause for celebration. A time that will attract friends and a few enemies. Indeed, a great moment to celebrate however know this, before gold becomes attractive, demandable, and profitable, it must first be passed through the fire. It must go through several refining processes of being both hot and cold. Letting you know something good doesn't come so easily. It took time to becom the beautiful gem the world sees. When you wait patiently for what you want and things you deserve, you will surely see your harvest in a great way.

**To get the harvest you want, you need to focus your mind daily on the following:**

1. You Must Know Who You Are In God.

2. Know Who God Is.
3. Seek God In Prayer.
4. Believe In Yourself.,
5. Seek Advice From People Who Can Help You.
6. Focus On What's Important.
7. Be Content.
8. Dream Big.
9. Stay In Your Lane.
10. Hope For The Best.

From today forward, I want you to set priorities for yourself. Set achievable goals and work towards them. Wait patiently for your goals, stay focused on them, and be consistent. Renew your mindset. I pray this is the push you needed to move you to the next level in your life. I pray this daily devotional journal has really helped and transformed your life mindset. As mentioned, your 21-day devotional has been leading to a message to God. A message that would let Him know that you know exactly what it is that you desire from Him, and that you are ready to reap the harvest. For your final assignment, I want you to review your previous entries and compose a written prayer to God. Always remember, you are what you think you are. You can do all things through Christ that strengthens you.

# REVIVED

I pray that you completed this devotional with a different mindset than when you first started. I pray that you feel renewed and restored. I pray that you feel empowered, uplifted, and motivated. Most importantly I pray that you feel revived.

*Wilt thou not revive us again: that thy people may rejoice in thee?*

*Shew us thy mercy, O Lord, and grant us thy salvation.*

*I will hear what God the Lord will speak: for he will speak peace unto his people, and to his saints: but let them not turn again to folly.*

**-Psalm 85: 6-8**

## YOU ARE

- ✔ YOU ARE CREATED
- ✔ YOU ARE AWAKENED
- ✔ YOU ARE LIMITLESS
- ✔ YOU ARE A GOAL GETTER
- ✔ YOU ARE INTERESTED
- ✔ YOU ARE SEDULOUS
- ✔ YOU ARE CONSISTENT
- ✔ YOU ARE PURPOSED
- ✔ YOU ARE THIRSTY
- ✔ YOU ARE A GIVER
- ✔ YOU ARE POSITIONED
- ✔ YOU ARE STANDING
- ✔ YOU ARE RIGHTEOUS
- ✔ YOU ARE LOVE
- ✔ YOU ARE A THINKER
- ✔ YOU ARE DISCIPLINED
- ✔ YOU ARE FEARLESS
- ✔ YOU ARE STRONG
- ✔ YOU ARE CONTENT
- ✔ YOU ARE IN LOVE
- ✔ YOU ARE HARVESTED

## YOU ARE REVIVED

# Concluding Prayer

My prayer is that this book has not only motivated you, but that it also empowered you to chase after your dreams. I pray that your spirit man has been awakened and fed, and that you feel empowered to encourage and uplift others around you. I pray that this book was the first step to transforming you into the best you possible.

So many people are full of potential, but we fall in life because we fail to realize whose we are. In life, you are going to fall or have setbacks. The important thing is that you get back up and stand on the word of God. My prayer is that this journey has shifted you from thinking that you are powerless, limited, and constrained in growth, to believing that you are greater than you ever could have imagined. When you know you're true to yourself, gifts will begin to manifest and your gifts will make room for you. All of a sudden, things that were a no, will become a yes. People who had once doubted you will believe in you. The finances that you needed to make your dream a reality, will start pouring in from directions you never expected. You will possess a certain confidence that will allow you to break away from toxic individuals and toxic circumstances. God created us to be powerful so that we could face our problems and come out safe. With a renewed and empowered mindset, you will stop seeing your problems as something to run from. Instead, you will begin to see yourself as someone who's specially equipped to change the status of your situation by overcoming the enemy and his attack. After you come to the point of realization of how powerful your creator is, His vast capabilities, and the extent to which He can do many great things, you will be confident that you can face whatever problems arise. My prayer is that this book has aided you in that determination.

God declared that we would have dominion over all the living and non-living things He has created. This should be reassurance for us. That we should always see ourselves as champions and victors and that this was how we were created. Challenges are meant to stretch us in order to reveal just how far we are capable of going, and just how much we are capable of enduring. As long as you are in your comfort zone, you will want things to come easily and conveniently to you. Comfort zones are not ideal for Christian living because they build complacency and will make you stagnant in growth. We are designed to be problem solvers, not problem avoiders.

My prayer is that when the next storm comes your way, you will have all of the confidence to face it head on. I pray that you will feel encouraged and empowered to know that you have the authority to tell your storm to cease. You are created in the image of God, so your storm will have no choice but to cease. You will still face many disappointments, you will still fall, but rest assured, you will not fail. The enemy's attacks will test your strength, discourage you, and may even feel as though it is going to break you, but our father said that where two or three are gathered in His name He would be in the midst. So here I am with you, gathered in his name, declaring your triumph and claiming your victory. Releasing your shackles of spiritual anguish and bondage.

## -You Are Free

# Acknowledgments

I first want to thank God, for instilling me a passion to thirst for, and spread his word. I would like to thank my husband for continuing to support me in my journey to spread God's word. You have stayed by my side through thick and through thin. To my children, Davon, Tamara, Tye, and Lyfe, I thank you for helping me mature and develop into the woman I am today. You all give me the drive and the determination to make anything possible and all that I do is for you. To my parents, I am forever grateful for the love and instruction that you have provided me, and now provide my children. Your love convinced me that this world was mine for the taking, and showed me that I truly was worthy, and that I was selected to do great things. I want to say thank you to you.

Last but definitely not least, THANK YOU for going on this 21-day journey with me. I pray you received what you desired, and I pray that you invited the spirit of abundance into your life!

www.ingramcontent.com/pod-product-compliance
Lightning Source LLC
Chambersburg PA
CBHW030220100526
44584CB00014BA/1399